MACRAMÈ FOR BEGINNERS

The easy step-by-step guide to create 24 unique and modern Macramè models for your home and garden.

CONTENTS

INTRODUCTION

It might seem to you quite tricky to form a macramé yourself, but you'll be surprised by how easy it's to select up the various macramé knots. The three plant hangers described during this might look to you a touch impressive and sophisticated, but with this may see that by just following easy step instructions with detailed photos, you'll complete any of the plant hangers without difficulties. Simple diagrams with instructions show you ways to tie the essential knots and prepare you for any of the three final projects.

Handicrafts were always a really fundamental human activity; for, crafts are an integral part of human life. Few crafts like macramé can be fascinatingly absorbent and versatile. With the textile industry changing rapidly, there's a requirement to revive and replace the old craft into modern ways during this ever-changing marketplace for newer fashion.

Macramé as a facet of decorative knots permeates nearly every culture, but within those cultures, it can manifest in several directions. The carefully braided strings, with the help of a needle-like tool, became the item for shaping fishnets. Their use within the apparel industry has been spectacular and influential among the youth in making sandals, shoes, jewelry, etc. it's now used also with other products to fashion all types of lovely works of art.

Macramé is closely related to the fashionable youth thanks to its rapid climb, quick adaptability, and extensive uses. In its traditional forms, Macramé (is an Italian name given in Genoa-its home and place of birth) became one among the foremost common textile techniques.

The association between contemporary crafts and macramé has led to the invention of a variety of methodologies and integrative methods, common in most cases, within the content; therefore, the adapted techniques. Such advanced methods and integrative techniques reflect the accomplishment of macramé art and its development.

As a product of the artistic intervention of scholarly artisans, this human intellectual accomplishment became necessary to include modern architecture requiring the utilization of other materials for trendy artifacts. While macramé art has been created and used for onward creation in most cultures aimed toward achieving both practical and artistic appeal, their end products vary from one culture to subsequent. These innovations, however, are, by definition, integral parts of cultural growth and are the results of the macramé artisans' revolutionary accomplishments over the years. The utilization of decoration knotting distinguishes early cultures and reflected intelligence creation. It's an art that matches all ages and skills. Today, macramé is experiencing a Revival of the 20th century. Both men and ladies' transition to figure with their hands and build not just utilitarian pieces but also decorative ones.

This simplicity and sturdiness, given the importance of macramé, portrays macramé as just a sort commodity described from a noneconomic viewpoint thanks to its slow production design. Macramé, as a way, is filled with vitality, adaptable, and exploratory and in several respects in product creation and production lends itself for processing and handling. Macramé painting has been a highly valued talent from the earliest times around the world.

The journey of macramé production, traveled through Arabia during the 13th century, Turkey, and Spain during the Moorish conquest, spread to the remainder of Europe in the early 14th century. It was later introduced to England in the late 17th century.

Sailors and seafaring people are said to possess spread this art style everywhere the planet consistent with tradition. By the 1920s, macramé had reached its dormant period in China and America, making artifacts like flower hangers, skillfully made boxes and industrial containers.

Macramé has the additional advantage of embracing the self-expression cycle by establishing the underlying purpose concealed within.

CHAPTER 1: WHAT IS MACRAMÉ

Macramé is a form of textile clothing that involves not the typical method of weaving or knitting but using a chain of knots. It is believed that it started in the thirteenth century in the western hemisphere with Arab weavers. They tied excess strings and yarn at the ends of hand-woven fabrics for towels, scarves, and shawls on decorative ends.

Materials that are often utilized for Macramé are Cotton twine, hemp, yarn, or leather. While there are variations, most of the knots would be the square knot, although complete feasibility and double half hitches. Jewelry is usually developed by blending ribbons with diamonds, diamonds, rings, diamonds, or cubes. You have a look at the huge bulk of the friendship outfits exhausted by faculty kiddies, you will learn they will have been created through the use of Macramé.

Macramé is a fun craft that you can try, and you can start with a small budget. There are a lot of free or reasonable patterns available and some great how-to books to help get you started. This would surely be a perfect craft to get your children, grandchildren and everyone involved in.

Macramé in the New Century

History of Macramé Leather

Arabia is the home of macramé. The calfskin and different materials were utilized toward the finish of texture. Next, it went into Spain and Turkey. What's more, in the fourteenth century, holy places in France and Italy utilized raised area materials made with macramé. Some accept that North American mariners made different kinds of knots with this calfskin.

Later on, in the seventeenth and nineteenth centuries, the British received it and added to its general prevalence. A couple of years after this, America and China embraced it and utilized it to create style sacks, purses, flower holders, and different compartments. It, along these lines, turned out to be generally used for business purposes.

Different knots can be made with the macramé calfskin: these incorporate half knot, square knot, two-fold half hitch, and overhand knot. Curiously, a lot more knots can be made from these essential and famous knots. In China, there are Macramé knots known as "Good Luck" and "Monkey's Fist." Macramé materials incorporate cowhide, jute, shoelace, nylon, and rayon, among others.

Benefits of Macramé Leather

Because of the imagination that goes into the knotting of macramé, numerous individuals appreciate doing it for art. A few people accept that macramé is a symptomatic treatment for improving mental capacities, reinforcing arms and joints, improving focus, and quieting the brain. This, in any case, doesn't suggest that it requires no incredible creative skill. Utilizing macramé requires being feeling reflective and cautiously meshing the calfskin into knots and ropes. Macramé calfskin can likewise be used in many home and design items. Packs, attire, shoes, gems, entryway hangings, hanging bushels, and plant holders can be adorned with this great meshing.

At the point when utilized in wristbands, macramé looks stunning and characterizes your look. It further settles on an announcement about your choice of design extras, since it is a fundamental conviction that high-quality gems are regularly carefully made. For the most part, this excellent rope meshing is utilized to keep globules and gemstones together solidly and pleasantly. In like manner, it is flexible, adaptable, and versatile to numerous items. The flexibility of macramé makes it an ideal counterpart for bright gemstones and different dots that made armbands enchanting. Visit our assortments now for armbands made with macramé cowhide.

The Art of Macramé

For men and women who'd like to grasp how-to macramé, there's a range of areas available on the marketplace. Creating complicated knots that produce whole patterns that could likewise be transformed into exquisite bracelets, flower baskets, and decorative wall-hangings.

CHAPTER 2: MACRAMÉ TERMS

Of course, you could also expect that there are certain terms you would be dealing with while trying Macramé out. By knowing these terms, it would be easier for you to make Macramé projects. You won't have a hard time, and the crafting would be a breeze!

For this, you could keep the following in mind!

Alternating

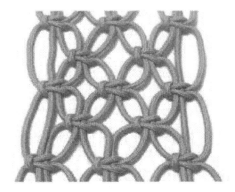

This is applied to patterns where more than one cord is being tied together. It involves switching and looping, just like the half-hitch.

Adjacent

These are knots or cords that rest next to one another.

Alternating Square Knots (ASK)

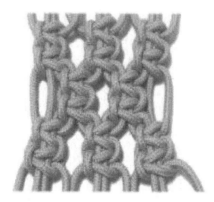

You'll find this in most Macramé patterns. As the name suggests, it's all about square knots that alternate on a fabric.

Bar

When a distinct area is raised in the pattern, it means that you have created a "bar". This could either be diagonal, horizontal, or vertical.

Bangle

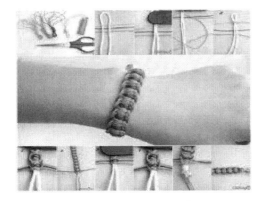

Bangle is the term given to any design with a continuous pattern.

Band

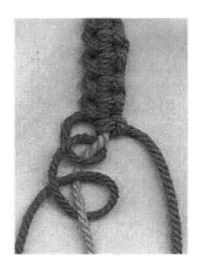

A design that has been knotted to be flat or wide.

Buttonhole (BH)

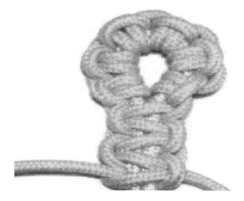

This is another name given to the Crown or Lark's head knot. It has been used since the Victorian Era.

Button Knot

This is a knot that is firm and is in a round shape.

Bundle

These are cords that have been grouped as one. They could be held together by a knot.

Braided Cord

These are materials with individual fibers that are grouped as one. It is also stronger than most materials because all the fibers work together as one.

Body

This talks about the main section.

Bight

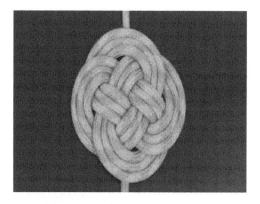

This is a section in the thread that has carefully been folded so loops could also make their way out to the knots.

Crook

This is basically just the part of the loop that has been curved and is situated near the crossing point.

Core

This term refers to a group of cords that are running along the center of a knot. They're also called "filling cords".

Cord

This could either be the material, or cord/thread that you are using, or specific cords that have been designed to work together.

Combination Knot

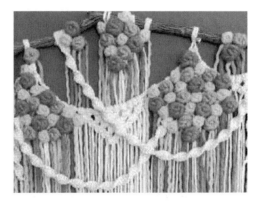

These are two knots that have been designed to work as one.

Cloisonne

A bead with metal filaments that is used for decorative purposes.

Chinese Crown Knot

This is usually used for Asian-inspired jewelry or décor.

Charm

This is a small bead that is meant to dangle and is usually just an inch in size.

Doubled

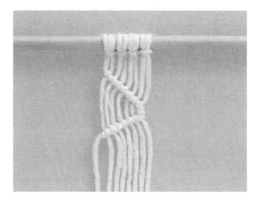

These are patterns that have been repeated in a single pattern.

Double Half Hitch (DHH)

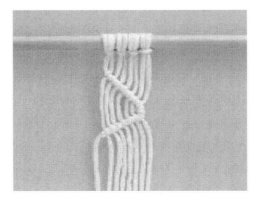

This is a specific type of knot that's not used in a lot of crafts, except for really decorative, unusual ones. This is made by making sure that two half hitches are resting beside each other.

Diameter

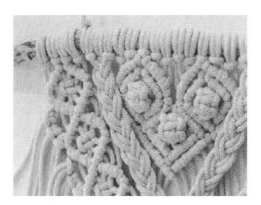

This describes the material's weight, based on millimeters.

Diagonal

This is a row of knots or cord that runs from the upper left side to the opposite.

Fusion Knots

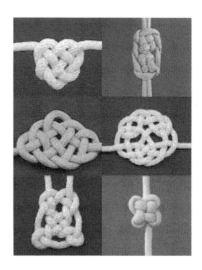

This starts with a knot so you could make a new design.

Fringe

This is a technique that allows cords to dangle down with individual fibers that unravel themselves along with the pattern.

Flax Linen

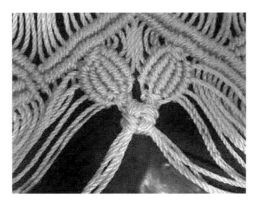

This is material coming from Linseed Oil that's best used for making jewelry, and even Macramé clothing—it has been used for over 5000 years already.

Finishing Knot

This is a kind of knot that allows specific knots to be tied to the cords so they would not unravel.

Holding Cord

This is the cord where the working cords are attached to.

Hitch

This is used to attach cords to cords, dowels, or rings.

Inverted

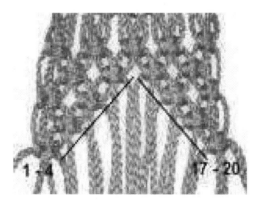

This means that you are working on something "upside-down".

Interlace

This is a pattern that could be woven or intertwined, so different areas could be linked together.

Micro-Macramé

This is the term given to Macramé projects that are quite small.

Metallic

These are materials that resemble silver, brass, or gold.

Mount

Mount or Mounting means that you have to attach a cord to a frame, dowel, or ring and is usually done at the start of a project.

Netting

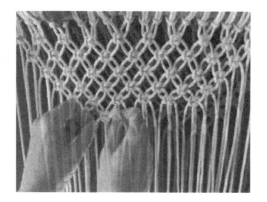

This is a process of knotting that describes knots formed between open rows of space and is usually used in wall hangings, curtains, and hammocks.

Organize

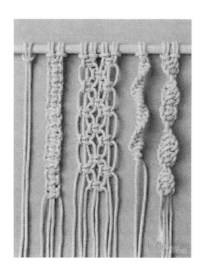

This is another term given to cords that have been collected or grouped as one.

Picot

These are loops that go through the edge of what you have knotted.

Pendant

A décor that you could add to a necklace or choker and could easily fit through the loops.

Synthetic

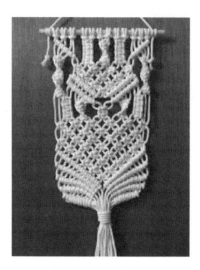

This means that the material you are using is man-made, and not natural.

Symmetry

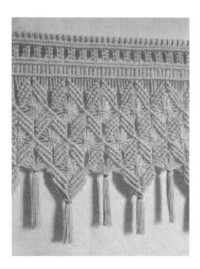

This means that the knots are balanced.

Standing End

This is the end of the cord that you have secured so the knot would be appropriately constructed.

Texture

This describes how the cord feels like in your hand.

Tension or Taut

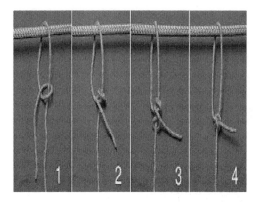

This is the term given to holding cords that have been secured or pulled straight so that they would be tighter than the other working cords.

Vertical

This describes knots that have been knitted upwards, or in a vertical manner.

Working End

This is the part of the cord that is used to construct the knot.

Weave

This is the process of letting the cords move as you let them pass over several segments in your pattern.

Tools and Materials

Yarn

The color part indicates a gathering of skeins that were colored together and along these lines have a similar shading; skeins from various color parcels, regardless of whether fundamentally the same in shading, are typically extraordinary and may deliver a noticeable level stripe when sewn together. If a knitter purchases thin yarn of a single-color parcel to finish an undertaking, extra skeins of a similar color part can, in some cases, begotten from other yarn stores or on the web. Something else, knitters can exchange skeins each couple of lines to help the color parcels mix simpler.

Metal Wire

There are different business applications for sewing texture made of metal wire by knitting machines. Steel wire of various sizes might be utilized for electric and attractive protection because of its conductivity. Treated steel might be used in an espresso press for its imperviousness to rust. Metal wire can likewise be utilized as gems.

Glass/Wax Sewn glass combines knitting, lost-wax throwing, shape-making, and oven throwing. The procedure includes:

knitting with wax strands, encompassing the woven wax piece with a warmth lenient headstrong material,

evacuating the wax by softening it out, hence making a shape;

setting the configuration in an oven where lead precious stone glass liquefies into the form;

after the way cools, the foam material is expelled to uncover the sewed glass piece.

Needles

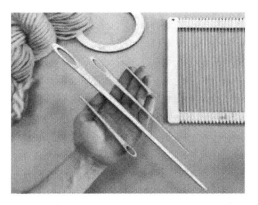

Various materials have grindings and unexpectedly grasp the yarn; smooth needles, for example, metallic needles, are helpful for quick knitting, while more unpleasant needles, for example, bamboo, offer more erosion and are this way less inclined to dropping join. The knitting of new lines happens just at the decreased finishes. Needles with lit tips have been offered to permit knitters to weave in obscurity.

Tape

Use tape on the ends of your cords to keep them from fraying. I suggest masking tape since it will not leave any marks on the cord. When cutting a cord, you can first put tape on the part where you are going to cut the cord. Cut in the exact half of the tape so that you will have the end and the beginning of the next cord with tape.

Clothes rack

To work comfortably, it is recommended to use a clothes rack. Any type of clothes rack will do, although one that is adjustable in height can be helpful. Something similar to a clothes racks can also work: a curtain rail or wooden step ladder might work just as well.

Cord

Cotton is very soft and pleasant to work with, while jute, for instance, could hurt on your hands while working with it. T-shirt yarn is cheap and quite easy to find. But you should take into account that most of the T-shirt yarn tends to be a bit elastic, which makes it less suitable for hanging objects which have to carry some weight like plant hangers.

Another aspect to consider is whether to choose a braided or twined cord. Braided cords are less prone to fraying, while the twined cord is much easier to fray.

Finally, consider the cord thickness: with a thicker cord, you will be able to create impressive, large-scale pieces, and with a finer cord, you can achieve a stunning intricacy in your patterns.

CHAPTER 3: BASIC KNOTS TUTORIALS AND TECHNIQUES

Main Knots Used

Square/Reef Knot. This is the primary knot used. This is done by binding the line or rope around a certain object. It is also known as the base knot. You could make it by tying a left hand over knot over a right hand. In short, right over left, and leftover right.

The Square Knot

Half Hitch. This is done by working the end of one line over the standing part of the knot. It is one of the most valuable components of knots, bends, and hitches, among anything else.

The Half Hitch

Overhand Knot. Another knot you could use is the overhand knot. It is known as one of the world's fundamental stitches and is especially helpful in Macramé. To tie, you could simply loop a thread to the end with the help of your thumb. Or, you could also twist a bight by placing your hand over your wrist as you loop. Use your fingers to work to the end.

The Overhand Knot

Crown Knot. Crown knot means that you have to go over the knot, go under twice, over twice, and under again. You'll then create something like what's shown on the illustration below.

Other Knots

Capuchin Knot

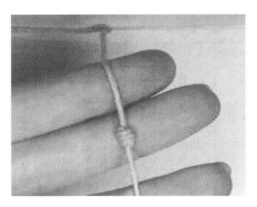

This is a great beginning knot for any project and can be used as the foundation for the base of the project. Use lightweight cord for this – it can be purchased at craft stores or online, wherever you get your macramé supplies.

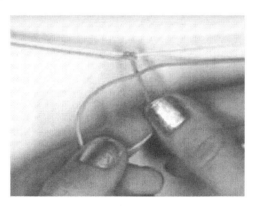

Observe the photos as you move along with this project, and take your time to make sure you are using the right string at the right point of the project.

Don't rush, and make sure you have even tension throughout. Practice makes perfect, but with the illustrations to help you, you'll find it's not hard at all to create.

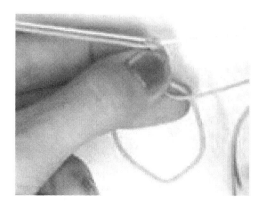

Start with the base cord, tying the knot onto this, and working your way along with the project.

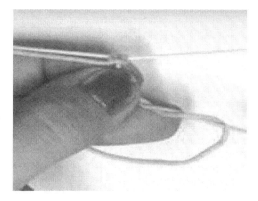

Twist the cord around itself 2 times, pulling the string through the center to form the knot.

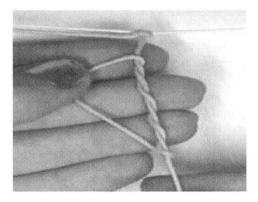

For the finished project, make sure that you have all your knots secure and firm throughout, and do your best to make sure it is all even. It is going to take practice before you can get it perfectly each time, but remember that practice does make perfect, and with time, you are going to get it without too much trouble.

Make sure all is even and secure and tie off. Snip off all the loose ends, and you are ready to go!

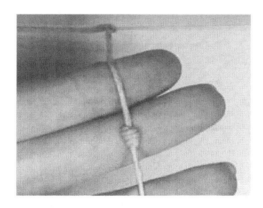

Crown Knot

This is a great beginning knot for any project and can be used as the foundation for the base of the project. Use lightweight cord for this – it can be purchased at craft stores or online, wherever you get your macramé supplies.

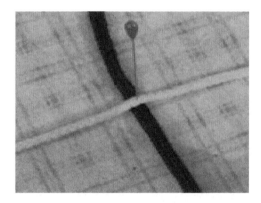

Observe the photos as you move along with this project, and take your time to make sure you are using the right string at the right point of the project.

Don't rush, and make sure you have even tension throughout. Practice makes perfect, but with the illustrations to help you, you'll find it's not hard at all to create.

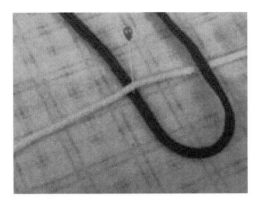

Use a pin to help keep everything in place as you are working.

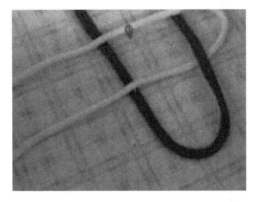

Weave the strings in and out of each other, as you can see in the photos. It helps to practice with different colors to help you see what is going on.

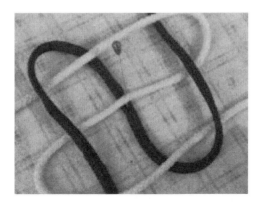

Pull the knot tight, then repeat for the next row on the outside.

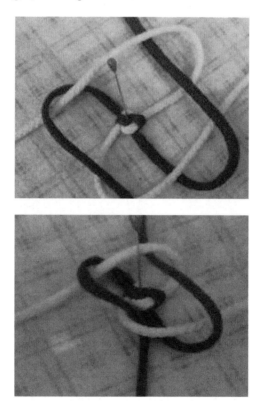

Continue to do this as often as you like to create the knot. You can make it as thick as you like, depending on the project. You can also create more than one length on the same cord.

For the finished project, make sure that you have all your knots secure and firm throughout, and do your best to make sure it is all even. It is going to take practice before you can get it perfectly each time, but remember that practice does make perfect, and with time, you are going to get it without too much trouble.

Make sure all is even and secure and tie off. Snip off all the loose ends, and you are ready to go!

Diagonal Double Half Knot

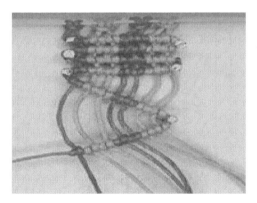

This is the perfect knot to use for basket hangings, decorations, or any projects that are going to require you to put weight on the project. Use a heavier weight cord for this, which you can find at craft stores or online.

Observe the photos as you move along with this project and take your time to make sure you are using the right string at the right point of the project.

Don't rush, and make sure you have even tension throughout. Practice makes perfect, but with the illustrations to help you, you'll find it's not hard at all to create.

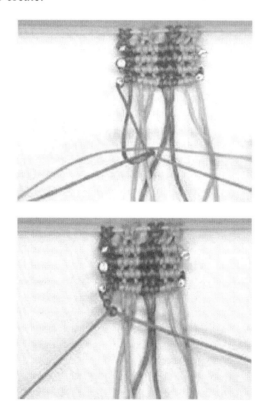

Start at the top of the project and work your way toward the bottom. Keep it even as you work your way throughout the piece. Tie the knots at 4-inch intervals, working your way down the entire thing.

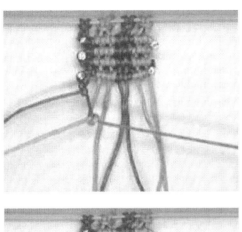

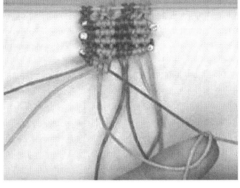

Weave in and out throughout, watching the photo, as you can see for the right placement of the knots. Again, it helps to practice with different colors so you can see what you need to do throughout the piece.

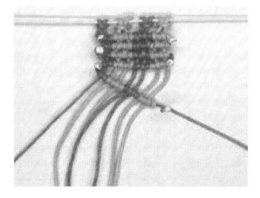

For the finished project, make sure that you have all your knots secure and firm throughout, and do your best to make sure it is all even. It is

45

going to take practice before you can get it perfectly each time, but remember that practice does make perfect, and with time, you are going to get it without too much trouble.

Make sure all is even and secure and tie off. Snip off all the loose ends, and you are ready to go!

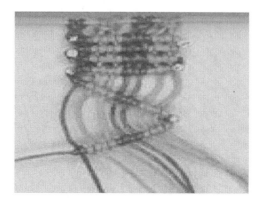

Frivolity Knot

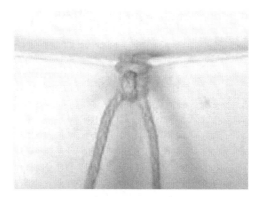

This is a great beginning knot for any project and can be used as the foundation for the base of the project. Use lightweight cord for this – it can be purchased at craft stores or online, wherever you get your macramé supplies.

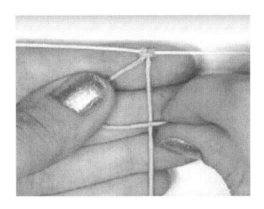

Observe the photos as you move along with this project, and take your time to make sure you are using the right string at the right point of the project.

Don't rush, and make sure you have even tension throughout. Practice makes perfect, but with the illustrations to help you, you'll find it's not hard at all to create.

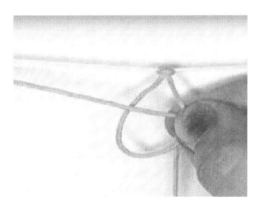

Use the base string as the guide to hold it in place, then tie the knot onto this. This is a very straight-forward knot; watch the photo and follow the directions you see.

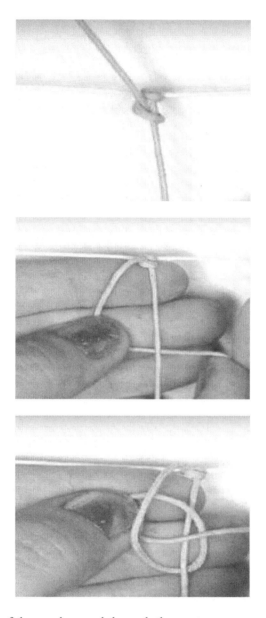

Pull the end of the cord up and through the center.

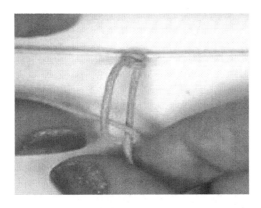

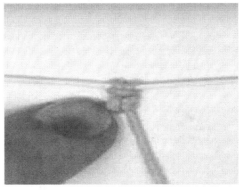

For the finished project, make sure that you have all your knots secure and firm throughout, and do your best to make sure it is all even. It is going to take practice before you can get it perfectly each time, but remember that practice does make perfect, and with time, you are going to get it without too much trouble.

Make sure all is even and secure and tie off. Snip off all the loose ends, and you are ready to go!

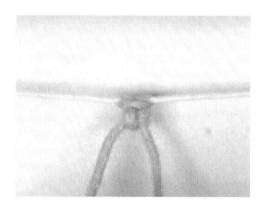

Horizontal Double Half Knot

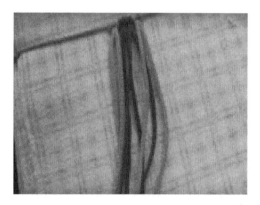

This is a great beginning knot for any project and can be used as the foundation for the base of the project. Use lightweight cord for this – it can be purchased at craft stores or online, wherever you get your macramé supplies.

Observe the photos as you move along with this project, and take your time to make sure you are using the right string at the right point of the project.

Don't rush, and make sure you have even tension throughout. Practice makes perfect, but with the illustrations to help you, you'll find it's not hard at all to create.

Start at the top of the project and work your way toward the bottom. Keep it even as you work your way throughout the piece. Tie the knots at 4-inch intervals, working your way down the entire thing.

For the finished project, make sure that you have all your knots secure and firm throughout, and do your best to make sure it is all even. It is going to take practice before you can get it perfectly each time, but remember that practice does make perfect, and with time, you are going to get it without too much trouble.

Make sure all is even and secure and tie off. Snip off all the loose ends, and you are ready to go!

Josephine Knot

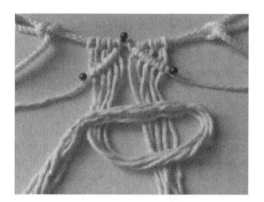

This is the perfect knot to use for basket hangings, decorations, or any projects that are going to require you to put weight on the project. Use a heavier weight cord for this, which you can find at craft stores or online.

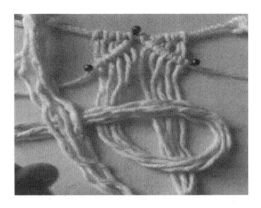

Watch the photos very carefully as you move along with this project, and take your time to make sure you are using the right string at the right point of the project.

Don't rush, and make sure you have even tension throughout. Practice makes perfect, but with the illustrations to help you, you'll find it's not hard at all to create.

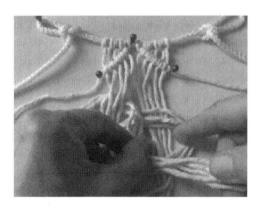

Use the pins along with the knots that you are tying, and work with larger areas all at the same time. This is going to help you keep the project in place as you continue to work throughout the piece.

Pull the ends of the knots through the loops, and form the ring in the center of the strings.

For the finished project, make sure that you have all your knots secure and firm throughout, and do your best to make sure it is all even. It is going to take practice before you can get it perfectly each time, but remember that practice does make perfect, and with time, you are going to get it without too much trouble.

Make sure all is even and secure, and tie off. Snip off all the loose ends, and you are ready to go!

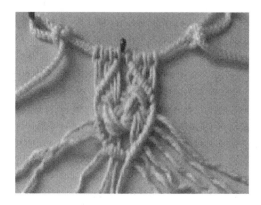

Lark's Head Knot

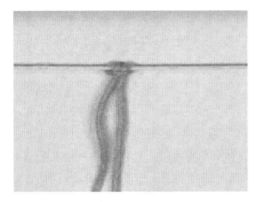

This is a great beginning knot for any project and can be used as the foundation for the base of the project. Use lightweight cord for this – it can be purchased at craft stores or online, wherever you get your macramé supplies.

Watch the photos very carefully as you move along with this project, and take your time to make sure you are using the right string at the right point of the project.

Don't rush, and make sure you have even tension throughout. Practice makes perfect, but with the illustrations to help you, you'll find it's not hard at all to create.

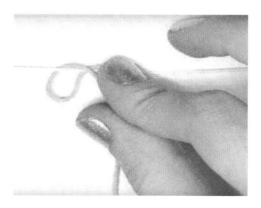

Use the base string as the core part of the knot, working around the end of the string with the cord. Make sure all is even as you loop the string around the base of the cord.

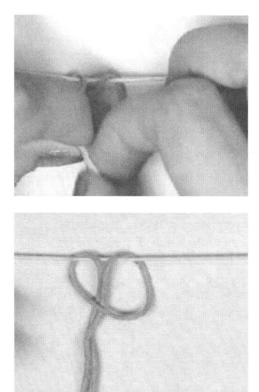

Create a slip knot around the base of the string and keep both ends even as you pull the cord through the center of the piece.

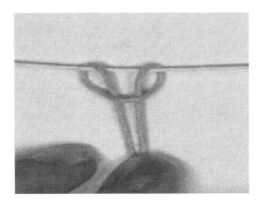

For the finished project, make sure that you have all your knots secure and firm throughout, and do your best to make sure it is all even. It is going to take practice before you can get it perfectly each time, but remember that practice does make perfect, and with time, you are going to get it without too much trouble.

Make sure all is even and secure and tie off. Snip off all the loose ends, and you are ready to go!

CHAPTER 4: HOW TO MAKE COMMON MACRAMÉ KNOTS AND PATTERNS

Different Knotting Techniques

Many Macramé tasks are easy to finish. Each job has a lot of models to create it your own. At any time you feel used to knotting, you are inclined to be in a position to produce your routines and make some genuinely exceptional cloths. Consider ways you can change a number of these Subsequent Macramé ideas:

- Wall-hangings
- Planters
- Crucial chains
- Hanging chairs
- Belts
- Antiques

Fringe on special fabrics

Millennials might have attracted Macramé's past, but individuals of ages can indeed love and fall in love for this particular craft.

Button square knots: begin out with three square knots. Then keep onto screw pliers by the back amid the horn cables before their original. Publish a rectangle under the bottom of this button to finish.

Cosmetic Dentistry: used making jewelry or to get Special knots such as Celtic and Chinese. These two approaches go perfectly with handmade jewelry and precious stones, for example, semi-precious stones, crystals, or pearls. These Macramé knots usually are intricate and could have a while to know.

Double-hitch knot: that Macramé knot is created by Generating two half hitch knots you afterward a second. Yank on the knots attentively.

Half Hitch knot: place Inch cable through your job Area (pin, therefore, that the cable will not proceed). At the finish of the cable that's been hauled across, the unmoving cable is drawn under the cable and pulled the loop which has been shaped.

Half knot: One of the normal Macramé knots to create. A fifty% knot is an ordinary knot; you start with four strings. Put it using this loop produced by the center cable together with your hand cable. Tug to Fasten the knot.

Overhand knot: Just One of the Most Often used knots in Macramé. Start with developing a loop by way of one's own cable. Pull the knot carefully.

Square knots: construct out of this fifty-five percent knot to Produce the square knot. Take your righthand cable behind the center strings and then send it about the left-handed cable. Only choose the left-handed cable and place it throughout the ideal hand by simply moving the middle strings and pull.

Ever wanted to be able to make your bracelets & designer handbag, but did not comprehend just how or did not have the appropriate resources? You have probably experienced such difficulty. Well, macramé design is exactly what the physician ordered.

Macramé is just a sort of fabric that works by using knotting. Materials that are utilized from the macramé process comprise jute, linen, strings got out of cotton twine, yarn, and hemp. It's a procedure for knotting ropes codes or strings collectively with one another to check something. This item might be described as necklace jewelry, necklace, etc. Macramé designs can be made complicated if different knots have been united to produce one layout or complicated.

A macramé bracelet can be made under:

Desired materials a Razorblade, a pencil or polyurethane Plank, or t-pin, a hemp cable, and sometimes some series of somebody else's taste.

Guidelines

Step 1: Measure Inch that the circumference of the wrist will probably soon be Measured. Afterward, cut two bits of this hemp rope together with the assistance of the scissors. The bits cut needs to be two times the magnitude of this wrist or the circumference measured initially. As an instance, when the dimension got was 5 inches, two strands measuring 15 inches per needs to be trimmed.

Step 2: Measure 2 strand is folded to around 30 minutes. Holding The pencil at a flat place, the strand is likely to probably be reverted onto the pen's cone to possess a loop just on the leading portion of stand, also, to guarantee loose finishes do hang. These ends ought to be passed via the loop and firmly pulled. This procedure ought to be replicated with yet another strand too. In the very long term, you'll have to get four strands hanging this particular pencil. Mentally, you might label these strands from side to left side, only 1 2. It's likely to work with whatever tagging procedure you locate easily.

Step 3: Measure 3 strand Inch ought to be obtained, on the other hand, significantly more than just two strands 2 and strand 3 (that in personality will be stranded at the center), and then below strand 4.

Step 4: Select strand 4 supporting the two Strands 3 and 2, throughout the loop that strand inch did form. To be certain, a half square rectangle is achieved, carefully pull strand 1 and strand 4.

Step 5: Now, you need to know a strand Constituting process. Take with this particular strand crossing process until fundamentally the bracelet accomplishes this particular period, which you can so desire. Spirals will probably be formed in both square knots because you carry on working out.

Step 6: the loops have been slid off the pen. After That, pull strand 2 and strand 3 to have the ability to lower the magnitude in these loops shaped only a small bit. Each of those four strands may then hold together along with two knots attached, like a way of procuring the job. These knots are crucial. Those strings which you side-by-side should subsequently be trimmed and this also should attentively be performed since close those knots as you possibly can.

Step 7 in the time you have obtained the bracelet set on your wrist. The-knot needs to be passed via the fold, therefore, to keep up the bracelet onto your wrist.

The measures above will allow you to design a straight-forward macramé bracelet. This macramé approach uses knotting instead of a weaving or knitting process. You may utilize beads to craft a beaded macramé necklace. You'll design distinguishing forms of decorations with macramé strategy. This is dependent upon you personally.

Fantasy catchers have gotten remarkably popular, and so they're extended in an enormous variety of styles and layouts. It's likely to uncover crotchet, woven or knotted dream-catchers. Macramé is a material making procedure that is based on knotting in the place of knitting or weaving. It's a French saying that ostensibly means knot since it's on the list of very first art-forms there is. The main knots within this procedure are square knots.

Macramé is a technique That's Been used for its Maximum period to decorate and craft numerous goods. You'll detect magnificent among a sort macramé handbag, wall-hangings, fantasy catchers, and a good deal of longer. It isn't too complicated to produce your macramé dream house, particularly the moment you have a couple of guides to take you through these knots. At any time, you have mastered the knotting; you're getting to be astounded by just how creative you can acquire.

The Strings

The strings are the most significant things you are likely to have to generate your piece. Cotton twine strings would be one of the most common due to the complete appearance they furnish, and you're getting to be in a posture to select unique colors to generate a design that fits with your taste. Besides cotton, then it's very likely to choose many substances, for example, cotton, linen, silk, and jute, determined by the kind of structure that you would like to realize. Numerous those cable chemicals are a ton easier for cosmetic purposes on the fantasy catcher than they genuinely are correct in creating a comprehensive slice.

Cord structure may potentially be a 3-ply value. It consists of three different spans of fiber to produce a robust and superbly shaped fantasy catcher.

The Rings

Macramé fantasy catchers can be accomplished with just wooden joints; nevertheless, in some specific scenarios, you could like to consider account a dowel determined by the dimensions of one's own thing. A decorative or metallic dowel may conduct the task well in offering you a fantastic surface to disperse a large number of strings, and that means that you may readily control them to accomplish your favorite design in the very long haul. If you'd really like to produce smaller sized ones, a push board, maybe whatever you need to begin on work.

Decorations

Despite macramé fantasy catchers, it's extremely potential that you simply incorporate jewelry along with other cosmetic capabilities in the own piece. You're able to tie the ribbons using Different strand colors, or maybe you include different necklaces, beads, and Cubes to make points of interest inside your design. It's likely to utilize right Hooks, u-pins, or upholstery for preserving the decorations and strings put up. If You Would like to use beads as Well as another accessory, then you should pick strand thickness attentively; preferably thick strand can Not provide this alluring appearance using attachments. Thinner strings make it to Be potential for the decorations to stick out from elegance.

Mix and Match Knots to Create All Kinds of Patterns

The Square Knot and Square Knot Variations

The square knot is a very common and versatile knot that is used in macramé. Square knots can be tied in a sennet (a length of knots tied one after the other) or across many lengths of cords to create solid or netting like patterns. Each knot is made using two steps and needs a minimum of three cords. Two cords are needed for tying the knots, and a further cord is needed to knot around. The following tutorial shows you how to tie a basic square knot using four cords and then how to use the knot in various forms.

Beads can be added to the knotting cords as you tie. They can also be threaded onto the central cords and then the knotting cords can be carried around them. For very large holed beads, all the cords can be passed through the beads. The square knot can be tied individually or in sennets. Using two different colored cords will produce a simple pattern through the sennet. This knot can also be tied in various formations to achieve decorative and more complex looking patterns for jewelry making and other items. This guide contains photographs showing how to tie a basic square knot and then illustrates four further ways in which square knots can be used.

These steps can now be repeated to create as many knots as desired.

The Half Hitch Knot and Half Hitch Variations

The half hitch knot is another very common and versatile knot that is used in macramé. Like the square knot, it is relatively easy to learn and can be used to create a variety of designs. Beads and other items can easily be added to either the central or knotting cords to embellish your designs.

Half hitch knots can be tied in two different ways. The knotting cord can be tied either over-under-over the holding cord, or alternately it can be tied under-over-under the holding cord. I have included photographs showing both on the following pages. Either of these half hitch knots can be used to tie a variety of formations, and I have included step by step photographs for four of these in the following part.

This is a vintage knot that can be used to create wide flat knotted pieces that would be suitable for bracelets, belts, bag straps, and similar. The width of the finished piece is based on the number of central cords used.

CHAPTER 5: MACRAMÉ BRACELETS

Macramé Bracelet with Rattail Cord and Glass Beads

This tutorial provides step-by-step instructions with photos showing you how to create a simple beaded macramé bracelet with rattail cord and glass beads. This is a great tutorial for beginners, as it only requires knowing how to tie a half knot to complete.

Colors and beads can be substituted to suit personal tastes.

Materials List:

- 130cm length of 1mm rattail cord
- 1 10-12mm disk bead or button with a central hole (hole must be 1mm minimum)
- 10 6mm black glass spacer beads
- 3 6mm patterned glass spacer beads

Tools List:

- Macramé board and pins (optional)
- Ruler
- Scissors
- Lighter

Step 1 - Fold over the first 5cm of the shorter length of cord and lay in front of you. These are the central cords.

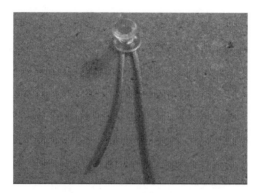

Step 2 - Fold the longer cord in half and place the center point underneath both cords.

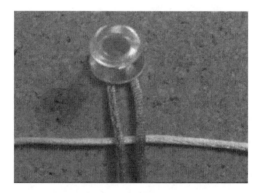

Step 3 - Starting with the left side cord tie one-half knot.

Step 4 - Tighten the knot fully and position it to create a 10mm loop at the end of the shorter length of the cord. This loop will form part of the bracelets fastener and needs to be a tight fit for the disk bead to fit through. Adjust as needed to suit your bead.

Step 5 - Always starting with the left side knotting cord, continue tying half knots until you have a Sennett 3.5cm long. The Spiral pattern can be seen, forming within a few knots. Pull the first few knots tied a little tighter than normal to hold the loop created in step 1 securely. The completed section of the bracelet, including the loop, should measure approximately 4.5cm.

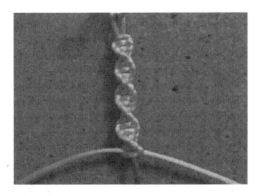

Step 6 - Thread one black bead, a patterned bead, and a second black bead onto the central cord and move these up to the bottom of the knots. Tie one-half knot underneath the beads to hold them in place. This knot should not be too tight. The beads should be sitting freely with the cords around them, not squashed together.

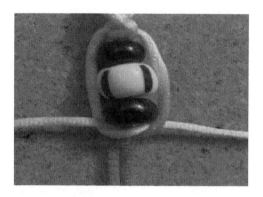

Step 7 - Tie a further four half knots.

Step 8 - Repeat step 6, this time adding one white, one black, and then a second black bead. Tie four more half knots.

Step 9 - Repeat steps 6-8 until all the beads have been added to the bracelet.

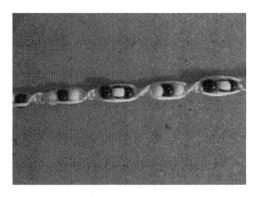

Step 10 - Continue tying half knots until you have a 3.5 cm Sennett to match the one at the beginning of the bracelet.

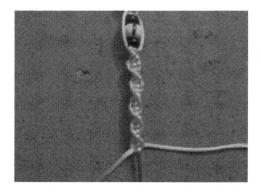

Step 11 - Cut off the excess knotting cords leaving a 3mm tail. Gently melt this tail using the lighter and fuse them to the final knot.

The melted rattail cord can get very hot and stick to skin, so it is best to use the point of the scissors, a needle, or similar item to carry out this step.

Step 12 - Thread the disk bead on to the central cord. Leave a gap of 3mm between the last knot and the bead and tie an overhand knot to secure the bead. Trim off the excess central cord and gently melt the end to prevent fraying.

Black and Red Macramé Bracelet

Step 1 - Fold the shorter red cord in half and lay it flat in front of you. These are the designs of central cords.

Step 2 - Fold the black cord in half and tie one square knot around the red central cords.

This knot needs to be positioned so that it creates a loop that the bead/flat button can pass through tightly. This forms the bracelets fastener.

Step 3 - Fold the longer red rattail cord in half and tie one-half knot around the red central cords underneath the black square knot.

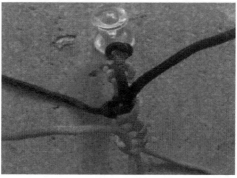

Step 4 - Tie a further four half knots, always starting with the same side cord so that the knots begin to form a spiral.

Step 5 - Carry the black cords over the red and tie one square knot underneath the half knots.

Step 6 - Pass the red cords under the black and tie five half knots.

Step 7 - Continue in this way until you have tied 18cm of knots.

If you have the bracelet pinned to a board or solid surface, the bracelet will twist as the form of the spiral, so you may find it easier to unpin and re-pin it as you work. The black cords should be flat; only the red knotting cords form the spiral.

Step 8 - Turn the bracelet over and trim away all the excess knotting cords leaving 3mm ends.

Step 9 - Gently melt the cord end with the lighter and press them against the knots.

Heated rattail cord becomes very hot and can stick to your skin and burn, so this step is safest carries out using a needle or scissors point to press on the melting cord.

Step 10 - Thread the flat bead/button onto the central cords. Push it up to the knots and leaving a 3mm gap tie an overhand knot to secure the bead. Cut off any excess cord and gently melt the ends to prevent fraying.

Fish Bone Macramé Bracelet

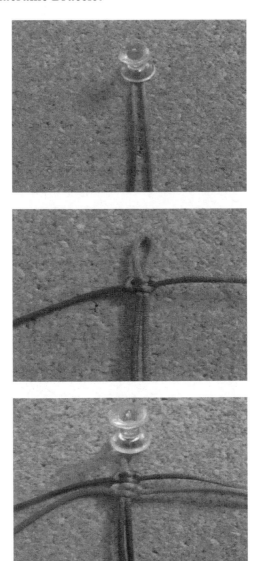

Step 1 - Fold the shorter blue cord in half and lay it in front of you.

Step 2 - Fold the long blue cord in half and tie one square knot around the shorter cord.

This knot should be positioned so that the loop created is a tight fit for the bead/button to fit through.

Step 3 - Use the red cord to tie a square knot underneath the bead.

Step 4 – Place a thread on the first bead.

Step 5 - Carry the blue cords over the red and tie a square knot underneath the bead.

Step 6 - Carry the red cords over and tie a square knot underneath the blue knot.

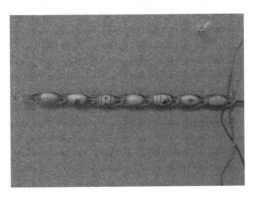

Step 7 – Place a thread on a second bead.

Step 8 - Repeat steps 5 and 6.

Step 9 - Continue in this way until all the beads have been added.

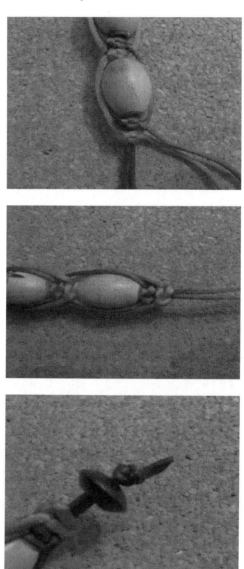

Step 10 - Leaving a 3mm tail cut off the remaining knotting cord on one side. Use the lighter to melt the ends and stick them to the back of the knots.

Take care of the melting cord as it gets very hot and can stick to your skin and burn. Use a needle or point of the scissors to press down the cord.

Step 11 - Repeat step 10 with the remaining cords.

Step 12 – Place a thread on the disk bead/button. Leave a 3mm gap between the final knot and the bead and tie an overhand knot.

Cut off any excess cord and melt the ends to prevent fraying.

Side by Side Macramé Bracelet

Step 1 - Gently heat the ends of each cord to make it easier to thread on the beads and prevent fraying.

Fold one cord in half and secure it to your macramé board (if using).

Step 2 - Fold a second cord in half and use it to tie one square knot around the cords on the macramé board.

Position this knot to create a small loop at the end of the first cord. This loop should be sized so that the flat bead/button fits through with a little pressure.

Step 3 - Fold the final length of the cord in half and use it to tie one square knot underneath the knot tied in step 2.

You should now have six cords, grouped in three sets of two.

Step 4 - Regroup the cords into two sets of three.

Step 5 - Working with one set of three cords, thread one bead purple and one silver bead on to the outer cords.

Step 6 - Using these two outer cords, tie one square knot around the central cord below the beads.

Step 7 - Thread two more beads on to the outer cords and place them below the two already added to the bracelet.

Tie one square knot around the central cord below the beads.

Step 8 - Repeat step 7 until all the purple and silver beads have been added to the bracelet.

Step 9 - Return to the beginning of the bracelet. Thread the cord nearest to the row of silver beads through the first silver bead.

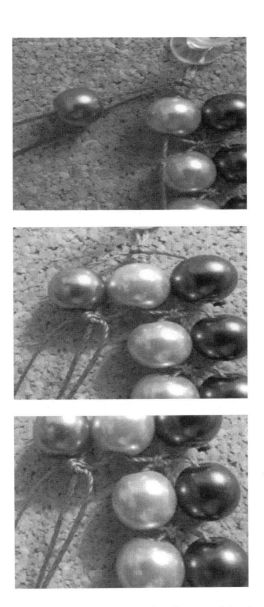

Step 10 - Thread one lilac bead onto the first cord in the set of three. This is the cord furthest from the beads.

Step 11 - Position this bead in line with the beads already added to the bracelet and tie one square knot beneath it.

Step 12 -. Thread the cord through the second silver bead. Add one lilac bead to the first cord and tie one square knot underneath it.

Step 13 - Repeat step 12 to add the lilac beads to the bracelet.

Step 14 - Separate the cords into three sets of two again.

Step 15 - Use the four outer cords to tie two square knots around the two central cords.

Step 16 - Turn the bracelet over and trim off the two sets of outer cords, leaving a 3mm tail.

Step 17 - Gently melt the cord ends and fuse them to the back of the knot.

Take care with this step as the melting cord is hot and can stick to your skin.

The point of the scissors can be used to press it into play.

Step 18 - Thread the disk bead/button onto the remaining two cords. Leaving a gap of 2mm between the last square knot and the bead, tie an overhand knot to secure. Trim off any excess cord and gently heat the end to prevent it fraying.

Macramé Necklaces

Silky Purple Necklace

This silky necklace looks quite majestic as it is in the color of purple. With the help of rhinestones, it becomes all the more elegant!

What you need:

- Rhinestones
- Clasp
- 2 inches of chain
- Thread and needle (in the same color scheme)
- 6 yards silk rattail cord

Instructions:

Cut string into 6 yards, and the other to be 36 inches. Make sure that you loop the last chain link.

Make use of square knots to tie the outer cord with the inner cord, and make sure to overlap on the left. Bring the string's end right under the center strings—knot by pulling the right and left ends of the cord.

Repeat the process on the opposite side of the chain and make sure to pull tight through the loop and make use of square knots until you reach your desired length.

Double knot the cord once you read your desired length so you could lock it up. Make use of fabric glue to secure the ends of the cord together.

Attach rhinestones with glue and let dry before using.

Enjoy your new necklace!

Leathery Knotted Necklace

A leather necklace has that rustic and earthy feel. Now, if you want to add some edge to an already beautiful thing, you could try Macramé and go and knot the thread!

What you need:

- Pliers
- Scissors
- Chain
- Crimp ends
- Jump rings
- Clasp
- 7 silver beads
- 5 meters of leather cord

Instructions:

Cut leather into a meter each and make 4 parts, then make a four-strand braid out of it.

Make use of the square knot to secure the loops—copy on the left side of the cord.

Add beads after you have done the first two knots. Hold it as you hold the right string. Create an empty knot, loop, and add some beads again.

Secure both ends of the cord using the crimp end. You could also use glue to keep it all the more secure.

Attach a piece of the chain at the end with a jump ring so your necklace could be ready.

Enjoy your new necklace!

CHAPTER 6: MACRAMÉ PLANT HANGERS

Macramé Plant Hanger Beginner

Description: Plant hanger of 2 feet and 5.5 inches (75 cm)

Knots: Square knot, alternating square knot, half a knot, and gathering knot.

Supplies:

- Cord: 10 strands of a cord of 18 feet and 0.5 inches (5,5 meter), 2 strands of 3 feet and 3.3 inches (1 meter)
- Ring: 1 round ring (wood) of 1.6 inches (4 cm) diameter
- Container: 7 inches (18 cm) diameter

Directions (step-by-step):

1. Fold the 10 long strands of cord in half through the wooden ring.

2. Tie all (now 20) strands together with 1 shorter strand with a gathering knot. Hide the cut cord ends after tying the gathering knot.

3. Make a square knot using all cords: use from each side 4 strands to make the square knot; the other 12 strands stay in the middle.

4. Divide the strands into 2 sets of 10 strands each. Tie a square knot in each set using 3 strands on each side (4 strands stay in the middle of each group).

5. Divide the strands into 3 sets of 6 strands for the outer groups and 8 strands for the group in the middle. Tie a square knot in each set using 2 strands on each side.

6. Divide the strands into 5 sets of 4 strands each and make a square knot with each set.

7. Continue with the 5 sets. In the 2 outer sets, you tie 4 square knots, and in the 3 inner sets, you tie 9 half knots.

8. Using all sets tie 7 alternating square knots by connecting two strands in each set with the right two strands of the set to it. In the first, third, fifth, and seventh row, you are not using the 2 outer strands on each side.

9. Repeat step 7 and 8. In repeating step 8 you tie 5 alternating square knots instead of 7 alternating square knots.

10. To help you with the steps, number the strands from left to right, numbering them no.1 to no. 20.

11. With the 4 middle strands (no. 9 tot 12) you make 14 square knots.

12. Make a square knot with the set of 4 strands no. 3 to 6 and the set of 4 strands no. 15 to 18.

13. Divide the strands into 4 sets of 4 strands (ignore the set with the 14 square knots in the middle) and tie 12 square knots in each set.

14. Dropdown 2 inches (5 cm).

15. Make 5 sets in the following way and tie in each set a square knot:

a. Set 1 consists out of strands no. 5, 6, 1 and 2

b. Set 2 consists out of strands no. 3, 4, 9 and 10

c. Set 3 consists out of strands no. 7, 7, 13 and 14

d. Set 4 consists of strands no. 11, 12, 17 and 18

e. Set 5 consists of strands no. 19, 20, 16 and 15

16. Dropdown another 2 inches (5 cm), no knots. This is the moment to place your chosen container/bowl into the hanger to make sure it will fit. If you need to leave more space without knots to fit your container, you can do so.

17. Gather all strands together and then tie a gathering knot with the leftover shorter strand. Trim all strands at different lengths to finish your project.

Happy Go Lucky Plant Hanger

What you will need:

You are going to need 1 ball of medium weight macramé cord in the color of your choice. You are also going to need scissors and any other pieces you want to use for decorations.

Directions:

Begin by separating the lengths of cord into 3 groups of 3 lengths each. You are going to begin bundling each group of three, then start braiding these lengths. Keep the braids nice and tight to make sure they get a twist to them, working your way down until you have a length that is 1 foot long for each braid.

There is going to be lengths of cord after the braid, and you are going to use these to create the length of the hanger.

Mark 1/2 of the way down your vase with marker, around each side of the vase. You are going to need to do this 4 times around the sides, then once more around the bottom.

You are going to hold the cords against your pot as you tie the knots, using this as a guide to see where to place the knots properly. When you are happy with the placement of each one, you are going to tie a final knot on the bottom to hold the pot in place.

If you want more stability at the base of the hanger, make a base as you would for the basket. Sew in place securely, and you are done!

To Assemble:

You are going to fit this to the size of the pot you are using – so make sure that your hanger is going to fit the pot as you tie the knots.

Fit the hanger around your pot, and make sure it is secure enough that the pot won't slip through. Tie the ropes around the top, securing it to a ring to hang the pot.

Then, hang where you like, and you are done!

Going Green Plant Hanger

What you will need:

You are going to need 1 ball of medium weight macramé cord in the color of your choice. You are also going to need scissors and any other pieces you want to use for decorations.

Directions:

Begin by separating the lengths of cord into 3 groups of 3 lengths each. You are going to begin bundling each group of three, then start braiding these lengths. Keep the braids nice and tight to make sure they get a twist to them, working your way down until you have a length that is 1 foot long for each braid.

There is going to be lengths of cord after the braid, and you are going to use these to create the length of the hanger.

Mark 1/4 of the way down your vase with marker, around each side of the vase. You are going to need to do this 4 times around the sides, then once more around the bottom.

You are going to hold the cords against your pot as you tie the knots, using this as a guide to see where to place the knots properly. When you are happy with the placement of each one, you are going to tie a final knot on the bottom to hold the pot in place.

If you want more stability at the base of the hanger, make a base as you would for the basket. Sew in place securely, and you are done!

To Assemble:

You are going to fit this to the size of the pot you are using – so make sure that your hanger is going to fit the pot as you tie the knots.

Fit the hanger around your pot, and make sure it is secure enough that the pot won't slip through. Tie the ropes around the top, securing it to a ring to hang the pot.

Then, hang where you like, and you are done!

Macramé Plant Hanger Intermediate

Description: Plant hanger of 4 feet and 3 inches (1,30 meter)

Knots: Square knot, alternating square knot, half a knot, alternating half hitch, gathering knot.

Supplies:

- Cord: 8 strands of cords of each 26 feet and 3 inches (8 meters), 1 short strand of cord
- Wooden Ring: 1 round ring (wood) of 1,6 inches (4 cm) diameter
- Container/Flowerpot: 7 inches (18 cm) diameter

Directions (step-by-step):

1. Fold 8 strands of cord, the long ones, in half over and through the ring. Now you have 16 strands of cord in total. Group them in sets of four strands.

2. Tie 4 square knots on each set of four strands.

3. Dropdown 3.15 inches (8 cm).

4. Tie 4 strands in each set with the right two of the set to it. Repeat on each of the 4 sets.

5. Dropdown 4.3 inches (11 cm).

6. Repeat step 4, starting with the 2 right strands this time.

7. Take 2 strands of 1 set and make 10 alternating half hitch knots. Repeat for the 2 left strands of that set. Repeat for all sets.

8. Dropdown 3.9 inches (10 cm) and tie a row of 48 half knots on each set of four strands.

9. Take the 2 middle strands of each set and make 8 alternating half hitch knots. You leave the 2 strands on the side of the set as they are (without knots).

10. Tie a row of 30 half knots on each set of four strands.

11. Use a new short strand of cord to make a gathering knot around all strands.

12. Cut off and fray the ends as desired.

Macramé Plant hanger Advanced

Description: Plant hanger of 2 feet and 5.5 inches (75 cm)

Knots: Square knot, alternating square knot, crown knot, gathering knot, and overhand knot.

Supplies:

- Cord: 4 strands of the cord of 13 feet and 1.5 inches (4 meter), 4 strands of 16 feet and 4.8 inches (5 meter), 2 strands of 3 feet and 3.4 inches (1 meter)
- Ring: 1 round ring (wood) of 1.5 inches (4 cm) diameter
- Beads: wooden beads
- Cristal Bowl/Container: 7 inches (18 cm) diameter

Directions (step-by-step):

1. Fold the 8 long strands of cord (4 strands of 13 feet and 1.5 inches and 4 strands of 16 feet and 4.8 inches) in half through the wooden ring.

2. Tie all (now 16) strands together with 1 shorter strand with a gathering knot. Hide the cut cord ends after tying the gathering knot.

3. Divide the strands into 4 sets of 4 strands each. Each set has 2 long strands and 2 shorter strands. Tie 5 Chinese crown knots in each set. Pull each strand tight and smooth.

4. Tie 8 square knots on each set of four strands. In each set, the 2 shorter strands are in the middle, and you are tying with the 2 outer, longer strands.

5. Tie 15 half square knots with each set.

6. Dropdown 5.5 inches (14 cm), no knots, and tie an alternating square knot to connect the left two cords in each set to it.

7. Dropdown 3.15 inches (8 cm) and tie an alternating square knot with 4 strands again.

8. Dropdown 1.5 inches (4 cm). Place your chosen container/bowl into the hanger to make sure it will fit, gather all strands together and then tie a gathering knot with the leftover shorter strand. Add a bead to each strand end (optional). Tie an overhand knot in each strand and trim all strands just below the overhand knots.

Various Ways to Use Macramé Plant Hangers

You can select a choice of plants that do well outdoors, and then make a series of plant wall mounts. You can make the plant wall mounts, and hang them someplace outside, like on a patio or terrace.

There is a range of various patterns and designs you can knit the wall mount in, so it is possible to tailor the look of the wall mount by doing this by utilizing various patterns. Some are more ornamental than others, for instance, while others are easier and plainer, and have a more spartan or practical look. Merely pick the pattern that can finest fit the space the wall mount is positioned in and begin to knit away!

Another excellent method to utilize macramé plant wall mounts is in spaces that benefit significantly from the peace and charm that plants can offer. Bedrooms can frequently be brightened up by the addition of a plant, and it is truly charming when you have a good plant in your bedroom if you invest an excellent quantity of time in there.

CHAPTER 7: CURTAINS AND WALL ARTS

Amazing Macramé Curtain

Macramé Curtains give your house the feel of that beach house look. You do not even have to add any trinkets or shells—but you can if you want to. Anyway, here is a great Macramé Curtain that you can make!

- Laundry rope (or any kind of rope/cord you want)
- Curtain rod
- Pins
- Lighter
- Tape

Tie four strands together and secure the top knots with pins so they could hold the structure down.

Take the strand on the outer right part and let it cross over to the left side using passing it through the middle. Tightly pull strings together and reverse what you have done earlier.

Repeat crossing the thread over four more times for the thread you now have in front of you. Take the strand on the outer left and let it pass through the middle, and then take the right and let it cross over the left side. Repeat as needed, then divide the group of strands to the left and to the right. Repeat until you reach the number of rows you want.

You can now apply this to the ropes. Gather the number of ropes you want—10 to 14 is okay, or whatever fits the rod, with good spacing. Start knotting at the top of the curtain until you reach your desired length. You can burn or tape the ends to prevent them from unraveling.

Braid the ropes together to give them that dreamy, beachside effect.

That is it; you can now use your new curtain!

Macramé Wall Art

Adding a bit of Macramé to your walls is always fun because it livens up space without making it cramped—or too overwhelming for your taste. It also looks beautiful without being too complicated to make. You can check it out below!

- Large wooden beads
- Acrylic paint
- Painter's tape
- Paintbrush
- Wooden dowel
- 70 yards rope

Attach the dowel to a wall. It is best just to use removable hooks, so you will not have to drill anymore.

Cut the rope into 14 x 4 pieces, as well as 2 x 5 pieces. Use 5-yard pieces to end the dowel with. Continue doing this with the rest of the rope.

Then, start making double half-hitch knots and continue all the way through, like what is shown below.

Once you get to the end of the dowel, tie the knots diagonally so that they would not fall or unravel in any way. You can also add the wooden beads any way you want, so you would get the kind of décor that you need. Make sure to tie the knots after doing so.

Use four ropes to make switch knots and keep the décor more secure. Tie around 8 of these.

Add a double half hitch and then tie them diagonally once again.

Add more beads and then trim the ends of the rope.

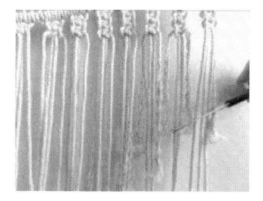

Once you have trimmed the rope, go ahead, and add some paint to it. Summery or neon colors would be good.

That is, it! You now have your own Macramé Wall Art!

Hanging Macramé Vase

To add a delicate, elegant touch to your house, you could create a Macramé Vase. With this one, you will have to make use of basket stitches/knots—you will learn about below. It is also perfect for those who love flowers—and want to add a touch of nature at home!

- Masking tape
- Tape measure or ruler
- 30 meters thick nylon cord
- Small round vase (with around 20 cm diameter)

Cut eight cords measuring 3.5 yards or 3.2 meters each and set aside one of them. Cut a cord that measures 31.5 inches and set it aside, as well. Then, cut one cord that measures 55 inches.

Now, group eight lengths of cord together—the ones you did not set aside, of course, and mark the center with a piece of tape.

Wrap the cords by holding them down together and take around 80 cm of it to make a tail—just like what you see below.

Wrap the cord around the back of the long section, and make sure to keep your thumb on the tail. Then, wrap the cord around the main cord group. Make sure it is firm, but do not make it too tight. If you can make the loop bigger, that would be good, too.

Do it 13 more times through the loop and go and pull the tail down so the loop could soften up. Stop letting the cords overlap by pulling them whenever necessary and then cut both ends so they would not be seen anymore.

Divide the cords into groups of four and secure the ends with tape.

Get the group of cords that you have not used yet and make sure to measure 11.5 inches from the beginning—or on top. Do the overhand knot and get the cord on the left-hand side. Fold it over two of the cords and let it go under the cord on the right-hand side.

Fold the fourth cord and let it pass under the leftmost cord then up the loop of the first cord. Make sure to push it under the large knot so that it would be firm.

Make more half-hitches until you form more twists. Stop when you see that you have made around 12 of them and then repeat with the rest of the cords.

Now, it is time to make the basket for the vase. What you must do here is measure 9 centimeters from your group of cords. Tie an overhand knot and make sure to mark with tape.

Let the two cord groups come together by laying them side by side.

Tie the cords down, but make sure to keep them flat. Make sure that the knots will not overlap, or else you would have a messy project—which is not what you would want to happen. Use two cords from the left as a starting point and then bring the two cords on the right over the top of the loop. Loop them together under the bottom cords and then work them back up once more.

Now, find your original loop and thread the same cords behind them. Then, let them pass through the left-hand cords by making use of the loop once more.

Let the knot move once you already have it in position. It should be around 3 inches or 7.5 cm from the overhand knots. After doing so, make sure that you flatten the cords and let them sit next to each other until you have a firm knot on top. Keep dividing and letting cords come together.

Next, get the cord on the left-hand side and let it go over the 2nd and 3rd cords before folding the fourth one under the first two cords. You would then see a square knot forming between the 2nd and 3rd cords. You should then repeat the process on the right-hand side. Open the cord on the right side and let it go under the left-hand cord. Repeat this process thrice, then join the four-square knots that you have made by laying them out on a table.

You will then see that the cords have come together at the base. Now, you must start wrapping the base by wrapping a 1.4-meter cord and wrap around 18 times.

To finish, just cut the cords the way you want. It is okay if they are not of the same length so that there would be variety—and they would look prettier on your wall. Make sure to tie overhand knots at the end of each of them before placing the vase inside.

Enjoy your new hanging vase!

CHAPTER 8: OTHER HOME PROJECTS

Sunscreen Macramé Holder

I'm so happy with this DIY because it means the sun finally comes out, and we need sunscreen! We purchased a sunscreen bottle with a carabiner last summer, which I clipped onto my pocket. It lasted the entire season and was perhaps the most significant discovery ever.

We have never lost sunscreen again, and without having to dig around in my bag, we could re-apply on the go. I missed the convenient travel sunscreen this summer, and I wanted to recreate it. I made this cool and inexpensive DIY macramé sunscreen holder because I love macramé so much, but you can also use it to bear hand sanitizer or lotion.

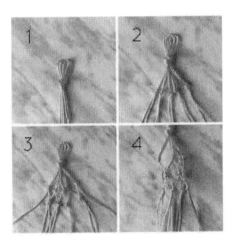

Direction

- Cord.
- Forklift.
- Sunscreen.
- Thin, empty flask.
- Bookmark.

- Clippers.
- Flash candle.

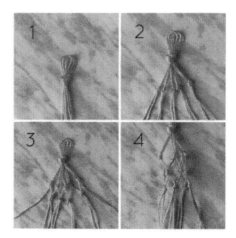

Guidelines

1. Cut five-string bits, about 20″ long.

2. Fold in half and tie the center of one big sweater. Tape down the knot to stay in place.

3. Divide the string into five pairs and knot each couple down to around 1″. Take another 1″ down, take one line, and knot it from the pair next to it with a loop.

4. Continue to cover the length of the bottle for about four rows of knots or. Slide your bottle in to test the fit and the appropriate number of knots. For ease of use, I put the bottle in the cap side downwards.

5. If the fit is right, tie the first knot to keep the bottle in place, with all the threads.

6. Place each string over a candle overheat to melt the ends and avoid fraying

7. Add a carabiner (or keyring) to the top knot to finish off, and connect to your pocket.

The travel size bottle last year was enough for us all summer, but you can replenish it as desired. You don't need to dig in your pocket now anytime you need a drop of sunscreen.

Arabian Nights Magic Carpet Rug

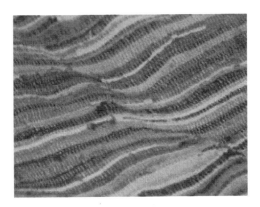

What you will need:

You are going to need 15 balls of medium weight macramé cord in the color of your choice. You are also going to need scissors and any other pieces you want to use for decorations.

Directions:

For this rug, you are going to make a variety of strips that you are then going to sew together into the rug shape. These are going to be 5 feet long for this rug, and you are going to continue with each strip the exact same way. Make sure they are all the same tension, and that they are all the same length.

You are going to do this according to your own color scheme. You can make the lengths the same color, or you can make them all different colors. Have fun with it, and keep going until you are happy with the amount of strips that you have. You can continue to add on, or you can stop when you reach the desired amount.

Maintain even stitching and tension throughout, and you are going to end up with a rug that lies flat. It takes time and practice so don't rush it too early.

To Assemble:

You are going to continue with each strip until you are happy with the color and size selection you have in place. Once you are happy with this, you are going to sew each of the strips together, sewing them into the square shape.

Once again, make sure you use tight, even stitches. You are going to go back and forth with each of the strips, sewing them together evenly and without leaving any gaps in between. Make sure that the edges are even with each other before tying off the last piece.

Snip off the loose ends, and you are done!

Inside Outside Rug

What you will need:

You are going to need 15 balls of medium weight macramé cord in the color of your choice. You are also going to need scissors and any other pieces you want to use for decorations.

Directions:

For this rug, you are going to make a variety of strips that you are then going to sew together into the rug shape. These are going to be 6 feet long for this rug, and you are going to continue with each strip the exact same way. Make sure they are all the same tension, and that they are all the same length.

You are going to do this according to your own color scheme. You can make the lengths the same color, or you can make them all different colors. Have fun with it, and keep going until you are happy with the amount of strips that you have. You can continue to add on, or you can stop when you reach the desired amount.

Maintain even stitching and tension throughout, and you are going to end up with a rug that lies flat. It takes time and practice so don't rush through.

To Assemble:

You are going to continue with each strip until you are happy with the color and size selection you have in place. Once you are happy with this, you are going to sew each of the strips together, sewing them into the square shape.

Once again, make sure you use tight, even stitches. You are going to go back and forth with each of the strips, sewing them together evenly and without leaving any gaps in between. Make sure that the edges are even with each other before tying off the last piece.

Snip off the loose ends, and you are done!

Happy in a Handbasket

What you will need:

You are going to need 12 balls of medium weight macramé cord in the color of your choice. You are also going to need scissors and any other pieces you want to use for decorations.

Directions:

You are going to use the cord directly, just as you would with the rugs. With this, you are going to begin braiding. Measure as you go, and braid enough until you can sew it into the base that you want for your basket.

When you are happy with the size, you are going to do the same for the strip around the top. Continue measuring as you go, until you are happy with the height of the basket. Tie off and set aside.

Create one final braid for the handle, and you are done!

To Assemble:

After you have sewn the base into a circle, you are going to add the strips to the side. Sew the side together, and when you are done, you are going to sew this side to the base.

Add the handle, and you are done!

A Tisket A Tasket It's a Woven Basket

What you will need:

You are going to need 12 balls of medium weight macramé cord in the color of your choice. You are also going to need scissors and any other pieces you want to use for decorations.

Directions:

You are going to use the cord directly, just as you would with the rugs. With this, you are going to begin braiding. Measure as you go, and braid enough until you can sew it into the base that you want for your basket.

Measure around the base, and begin weaving a strip that is equal to this length, you are going to continue going back and forth with this strip until it is as tall as you want it to then you are going to tie it off.

Fit this strip around the base once you have it assembled, then you are ready to add the handle.

Create one final braid for the handle, and you are done!

To Assemble:

After you have sewn the base into a circle, you are going to add the strips to the side. Sew the side together, and when you are done, you are going to sew this side to the base.

Add the handle, and you are done!

Sidekick Handbag

What you will need:

You are going to need 3 balls of medium weight macramé cord in the color of your choice. You are also going to need scissors and any other pieces you want to use for decorations.

Directions:

Using your cord, you are going to weave a rectangle that is 1 foot wide by 2 feet long. When you fold this, it is going to turn into a square – but of course you can alter this to fit you the way you want it to.

The strip you are going to weave the same way, but this time you are going to continue with a strip that is 3 inches wide and 6 feet long. Again, if you want to alter this one way or another, you are more than welcome to until it fits you the way you want it to.

When you are happy with the size of the piece, you are going to tie it off and set it aside until you are ready to assemble.

To Assemble:

Fold the body of the bag in half, and sew up both sides. Add the strip for the handle, making sure that it is secure to the body of the piece.

Snip off all the loose ends, and you are done!

Messenger Bag Deluxe

What you will need:

You are going to need 3 balls of medium weight macramé cord in the color of your choice. You are also going to need scissors and any other pieces you want to use for decorations.

Directions:

Using your cord, you are going to weave a rectangle that is 15 inches wide by 3 feet long. When you fold this, it is going to turn into a long square shape – but of course you can alter this to fit you the way you want it to.

The strip you are going to weave the same way, but this time you are going to continue with a strip that is 2 inches wide and 6 feet long. Again, if you want to alter this one way or another, you are more than welcome to until it fits you the way you want it to.

When you are happy with the size of the piece, you are going to tie it off and set it aside until you are ready to assemble.

To Assemble:

Fold the body of the bag in half, and sew up both sides. Add the strip for the handle, making sure that it is secure to the body of the piece.

Snip off all the loose ends, and you are done!

Macramé tote bag

This bag looks perfect for summer fashion, but it will also take you into the fall. Imagine sitting within a few squashes as you head home to be warm with some sort of spiced tea under a blanket. Enjoying the autumn.

Directions.

1. Cut the 2.3-meter long rope in 10 lengths. Split them in half and loop through the gap on the bag handle to the folded middle. Take the ends of the line and proceed through the loop you made in this earlier stage. Tight drive. Repeat this until five pieces of rope are tied to the handle of each container.

2. Starting at one end, split two sections of rope from each other and move the remainder sideways. With those two parts, we will make the first knot. This is the knot that we will use in the tutorial, so keep returning to the next few measures if you get stuck.

Let a right strand bend, so it crosses the correct angle over the left rope.

Take the rope on the left (which is still straight) and thread that you built with the two cords through the gap. Pull both ends of the line away before the knot is shaped and is in the right position. You want the handle to be about 5 cm forward.

Take the left-hand rope to complete the knot, and this time bring it over the right.

This time the right-hand rope is threaded through the crack. Turn the close tie over again. This is a double half hitch knot now complete.

3. Using the remaining ropes on the handle to make four more of those knots in a line. So continue again but skip the first rope this time, and the second and third knot. Go on down the line. This time, you'll make four knots, and there's no knotting of the first and last rope.

4. Render the third row the same as the first one (thus five loops, without losing any ropes) after you have finished the second row.

5. Repeat steps 2-4 on the second handle until the third row is done. If that's finished, but the two handle facing each other together with the back ends.

 6. Take the two end ropes from both the front and back of the bag and tie these together to start the next section. Knot the front and back ties, until you hit the other end. You will then be left in front and back of the last lines.
7. Keep knotting in this style until you are left with around 10 cm of rope on the ropes.

8. Split rope length 4 meters long. Using the same method that you used with handles to tie this into the last side knot.

9. Take one front and one back string, and loop the rope around them. Then take another two loops (one from the front and one from the back) and do the same thing. Act before you make it to the top.

10. Draw the rope which hangs down. Connect these threads to stay in place in knots. To strengthen these, you should apply some glue. Combine it to form a fringe.

And you're done with your pack if you want something to dip in a natural burnt red or sage green with a flavored pick.

Chapter 9: More Jewelry Projects

Macramé Gem Necklace

This one has that enchanting, beautiful feel! Aside from knots, it makes use of gemstones that could spruce up your look! Surely, it's one necklace you'd love to wear over and over again!

What you need:

- Your choice of gemstones
- Beads
- Crocheted or waxed cotton
- Water
- Glue

Instructions:

Get four equal lengths of cotton—this depends on how long you want the necklace to be.

Tie a base knot as you hold the four cotton lengths. Once you do this, you'd notice that you'd have eight pieces of cotton lengths with you. What you should do is separate them into twos, and tie a knot in each of those pairs before you start knotting with the square knot.

Tie individual strands of the cotton to the length next to it. Make sure you see some depth before stringing any gemstones along and make sure to knot before and after adding the gemstones to keep them secure.

Take four of the strands in your hand and tie a knot on the top side of the bag. Tie strands until you reach the length and look you want.

Knot the ends to avoid spooling, and use water with glue to keep it more secure.

Yarn Twisted Necklace

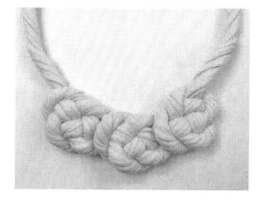

This one is quite simple as you can use any kind of yarn that you want, especially thick or worsted ones, to give your projects more flair and to make it modest—but wearable!

What you need:

- Yarn in various colors
- Water
- Glue

Instructions:

Cut two to four pieces of yarn—it's up to you how much you want.

Start braiding, and knot using the square knot. Make sure that you secure the pieces of yarn together.

Knot until your desired length, and then secure the piece with a mix of glue and water at the ends.

Nautical Rope Necklace

This one is light and easy on the eyes, and is quite edgy—literally and figuratively, without being over the top! It will also remind you of the sea—or the waves of the ocean!

What you need:

- Pendant with jump ring or bail
- Ruler
- Scissors
- White nylon cord
- Knotting board

Instructions:

Cut 7 feet or 84" of nylon cord.

Then, keep the strands together as a group. Tie an overhand knot around the two strings. Make sure there's 1 to 2" of space between them.

Make an overhand knot 6" away from the end. Tighten the knot by pulling individual strands and make sure to secure it on the knotting board. Separate the strands into two groups.

Take the left part of the cord and cross it under the right corner of the cord. Get the right cord group and cross it over the left side. Tighten as you pull down and knot until you reach 16 inches.

Check the last double chain and make an overhand knot. Tie them 6 inches from what you have created. Add a pendant, if you want, and make sure you knot before and after adding it to keep it secure.

Easy Macramé Ring

Macramé rings could work as friendship rings—which are perfect giveaways for special events, especially if you're doing them with your friends! It's also not that complicated to make—so make sure that you check this one out!

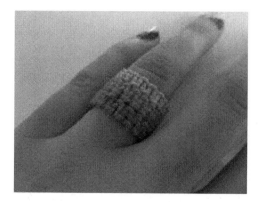

What you need:

- Glue
- Scissors
- About 1.20 m yarn
- Yarn in multiple colors
- Round object (just to get the size of your finger with)

Instructions:

Wrap yarn around the round object after folding it in half. Check if it has been divided equally, and then tie the ends with two knots.

Put the right strand over the left strand, and then let the left strand go underneath the middle. Keep knotting until you reach your desired length.

Pull the last knot tightly to keep it secure, and then run some glue over it to make it even tighter. Let it dry before holding it again.

Wear your ring and enjoy it!

Sun and Moon Anklet

Anklets add a bit of funk and fun in your style. This anklet will do that and more! It has that ethereal feel as it's made with sun and moonstones—making it all the more magical!

What you need:

- 16 mm sun/moon reversible bead
- 2 round 8mm rose silver beads
- 1mm 18-inch hemp
- 1-yard hemp (your choice of color)

Instructions:

Gather the strands together by holding them and then tie an overhand knot after leaving an inch of the tail.

Anchor the knot by slipping it to the ring. Braid around two inches and then make an overhand knot.

Arrange strands and then tie a 3-inch square knot. Slide the sun/moon bead in the area then make another square knot before adding a rose bead.

Continue with 3 more square knots and then tie an overhand knot. Do at least 2 inches of this.

Go and tie an overhand knot and trim an inch off the ends.

Let the "anklet" slip off the ring.

Enjoy your new anklet!

Macramé Rhinestone Ring

Now, this one is a pretty rhinestone ring that could also serve as a friendship ring. It's quite colorful, but the rhinestone keeps it toned down and elegant. Try it out by following the instructions below!

What you need:

- Embroidery floss (in four different colors)
- Scissors
- Gemstone
- Tape

Instructions:

Cut three lengths of each thread and tie all the ends together using an overhand knot. Tape down to secure. If you want to label the threads, you could do that, too, so that you would not get confused (i.e., A, B, C, etc.)

Now, take the bottom left cord and cross it above the top left cord.

Take the bottom-right cord and cross it above the top right cord.

Take the upper left cord and cross it above the bottom left cord.

Take the upper right cord and cross it above the bottom right cord.

Repeat the process on the other side of the cord, and then insert the rhinestone when you feel like it.

Pull the last parts of the cord tightly so you could keep them together.

Repeat the process until you reach your desired length, and tie ends together—glue to secure.

Macramé Watch Strand

If you're looking for ways to spice up your wristwatch, well, now's your chance! Make use of this Macramé Watch Strand Pattern, and you'll get what you want!

What you need:

- Jump rings
- Closure
- 2mm Crimp ends (you can choose another size, depending on your preferences)
- Embroidery or craft floss
- Watch with posts

Instructions:

Choose your types of floss, as well as their colors. Take at least 10 long strands for each side of the watch.

Lash each floss onto the bar/posts of the watch and thread like you would a regular Macramé bracelet or necklace.

Braid the ends tightly if you want to make it more stylish and cut the ends. Burn with lighter to secure before placing jump rings and closure.

Use and enjoy!

CHAPTER 10: OWL MACRAMÉ

For this project, you will need the different colored threads, as shown above: eye beads, one nose bead, and a sitting pole for the owl. The threads will be referred to by color, and the shorter pink thread will be called the short pink thread. You may need some pins to hold down your work throughout.

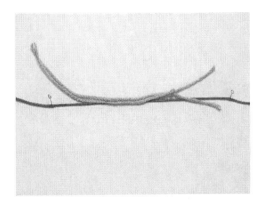

Step 1: Take both of the short pink threads and tie an overhand knot on the right end of the threads, as shown.

Step 2: Take both threads, now form a loop on top of the thread. This can be done by using your thumb as a guide to how long the loop should be. Then hold the thread at this length so that the loop is isolated.

Step 3: while keeping the loop isolated, create another loop with the rest of the threads and then place the original loop through the new loop while keeping hold of the original loop and then when through you can pull to tighten and you should end up with something like the picture above.

Step 4: Take your black thread and lay it down horizontally below the pink thread, as shown here. You can pin the thread down to give you more stability for the steps ahead. Some people really find this helpful.

Step 5: Take one of the pink threads and fold it in half. Place it behind the black and short pink threads that are already in place.

Step 6: A loop should have been created at the top of your pink thread. Fold this over the black and short pink threads. Now pull the end of the pink thread through the loop and pull tightly to secure. This will create a Lark's head knot (image above).

Step 7: Take one of your blue threads and create a Lark's head knot in the same way as previously shown. Make sure they are next to each other. If the step is followed correctly, it should look like the image above.

Step 8: Take three more blue threads and create three more Lark's head knots making sure you have two each side of the knot in the middle. The pink knot just created will act as the middle knot, so you will already have a blue on the right.

Step 9: After this is completed, take two pink threads and create a Lark's Head knot on the right and one on the left like in the image above.

Step 10: For this step, you will need to create two more overhand knots on the ends of Lark's head knots.

Step 11: Firstly, do this on the left side, ensuring that Lark's head knot is secured by the overhand knot.

Step 12: Now repeat this for the right-hand side. You can refer back to the previous instructions.

TIP: when creating the overhand knots, make sure you do not tighten the knot until it gets down to Lark's head knot then tighten to secure. Otherwise, you will end up with a knot in the middle of your thread.

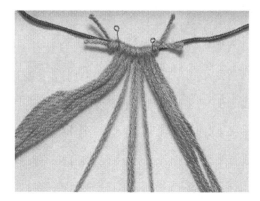

Step 13: Trim the ends of the thread left after creating the overhand knots. Make sure to leave around an inch of thread like the picture shows.

Step 14: Starting from the left, take two pink threads and three blue threads and pull them aside.

Step 15: Starting from the right, take two pink threads and three blue threads and pull them to the right. After completing this, you should have the threads left that are in the image. This should be two pink threads in the middle and one blue either side.

Step 16: At this stage, ignore the five threads, either side and focus on the four threads in the middle that you indicated earlier.

Step 17: Take the left blue thread, place over the two pink threads, and under the single blue thread on the right. Now take a right blue thread and place it under the pink threads and through the loop created by the blue threads. Simultaneously pull both blue threads and push the knot upwards to secure the knot in place. You can also pull the pink threads down to ensure they are hanging free. You will have created a half square knot.

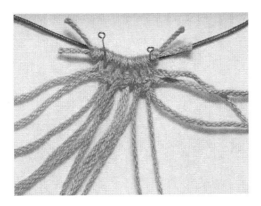

Step 18: Starting from the right group of threads, which consists of five threads. Skip the first thread on the right and proceed to create a half square knot as in the instructions above.

Step 19: Now go to the left side group of threads. Skip the first thread on the left and use the remaining four threads to, again, create a half square knot, and your macramé piece should look like the above.

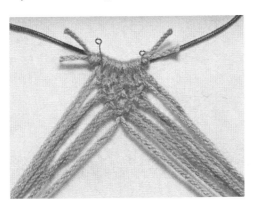

Step 20: Proceed to create two half-square knots under your three half square knots previously made and then create a single half square knot under your two. It should look like the image above. The instructions to follow are above.

Step 21: Separate your threads into two groups so that there is 7 in each one (4 blue, 3 pink).

Step 22: Firstly, for your left group of threads, take the first pink thread at the top and place it diagonally across your left group of threads. Then take the thread next to it and follow the instructions below.

Step 23: Loop it over the horizontal thread, under itself, then using the same thread loop it over the horizontal thread again and finally through the loop created. Pull to secure the knot tightly. You will have a half hitch knot.

Step 24: Now take the first pink thread on the right, place it diagonally across the group of threads. Take the thread next to it and repeat the steps above on how to create a half hitch knot.

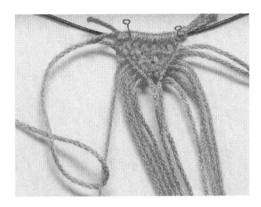

Step 25: Your threads should still be separated into two groups. From the group on the left, take the first pink thread on the top, the blue thread next to it, and use the pink thread to create 5 half hitch knots on the blue thread. Your image should look like the image below.

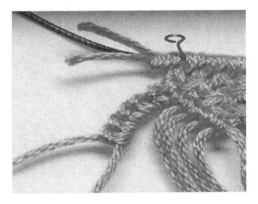

This is what the left side of your work should look like at this point.

Step 26: Here, proceed to complete a half hitch knot in the same way as described above but on the right side. Instructions above.

Step 27: Now, on the right side next to your half hitch knot, take the three blue threads and pass them through one of the eye beads and push to the top.

Step 28: Repeat this for the three blue threads on the left as well. Your macramé piece should look like the picture shown.

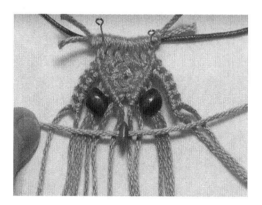

Step 29: Take a new pink thread from your pile. Put it through the nose bead so that the nose bead is in the middle. Then hover the thread over the piece making sure the nose bead is in the middle and then place down.

Step 30: Once you have the new thread horizontally on the piece. Take the first pink thread on the right and tie a half hitch knot around the horizontal pink thread.

Step 31: After tying the first half hitch knot with the pink thread, take the next blue threads and tie a single half hitch knot using each one. Then proceed to take the next two pink threads and tie a half hitch knot in each one.

Step 32: Before proceeding, ensure that the nose bead is in the middle and is placed exactly where you would like it. Now proceed to create a series of half hitch knots on the eight sides as previously explained. This should then look like the image below.

Step 33: If you pinned the work down earlier, you can take them out as your work should be stable enough as we proceed.

If you completed the steps as told, you should end up with your work looking like this. Your owl should be coming along nicely.

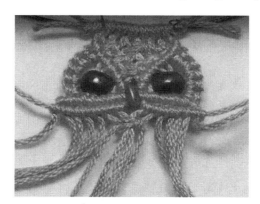

Step 34: Below your nose bead in the middle, you should have a pink thread on each side. Take the one on the left and place horizontally across the threads on the left. Tie half hitch knots from right to left, inclusive of all threads on the left.

Step 35: Secondly, repeat this for the right side.

Step 36: On each side of the owl's nose bead, there should be two half hitch knots.

Step 37: Take the 4 threads in the middle, which consists of two pinks in the middle and one blue either side. Now tie a half square knot using these threads.

Step 38: Use the previous instructions on how to create this knot.

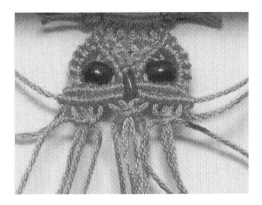

Step 39: Now, take the next four threads on the left of the half square knot just created in the middle and create another half square knot. Then repeat this process for the right-hand side. It should look like the picture above.

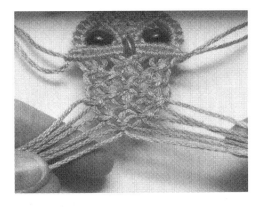

Step 40: Proceed to create more square knots under the ones just created so that you have three on the outer part of the owl. Below this creates a row of only two square knots. Then below this one, create on square knot below the two.

Step 41: Go back up the nose of your owl and look down at the half hitch knots. The second ones on the left and right will have a common thread running through them that also goes out past the knots and extends horizontally.

Step 42: From both the threads, attach 3 threads to the left one, using a lark's head knot. Out of the 3 threads, you attached 2 should be blue and 1 pink. Make sure you arrange, as seen in the picture above, as their arrangement is going to be the start of the wings of the owl.

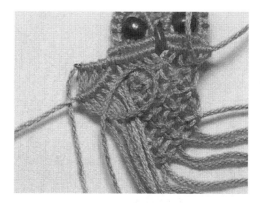

Step 43: From the wing of the owl, take a single pink thread from the right and place it horizontally across your threads and take the thread next to it and create a half hitch knot(loop the thread over the horizontal one twice and pull through the loop tightly to secure the knot). Repeat this with each thread from the left to right till your work looks like the image above.

Step 44: Now take the last pink thread and create another half hitch knot, as seen in the image above.

Step 45: Below our previous half hitch knot, take the first thread on the right and place it horizontally across your other threads and take thread next to the horizontal thread and create a half hitch knot, repeat for all the other threads on that row of threads.

Step 46: Continue creating rows of half hitch knots until you have 7 rows of them (the half hitch knots should progressively become more vertical as you go along. This is supposed to happen).

Step 47: Now, simply repeat what you have done on the right-wing on the left-wing.

If you have followed the steps correctly, your work should look like the image above.

Now that you have completed both wings, you are going to join the wings to the body of the owl.

Step 48: From the group of threads located on the body of the owl, split the threads into 2 even groups.

Step: 49: Take the left group and bundle them together, then on the left-wing take the first thread at the top and tie a half hitch knot around the bundle, continue this till you have used each thread to tie a half hitch knot once.

Step 50: Repeat the process above on the right side of the owl; this should result in a piece that looks similar to the image below.

Step 51: Take four threads from both sides of the wings, as shown in the right picture below, and wrap them around the pole stick, shaping the owl's feet (left picture below).

Step 52: Take the threads from the edges and tie four square knots around the rest of the threads to secure the sitting pole firmly (see the two images below).

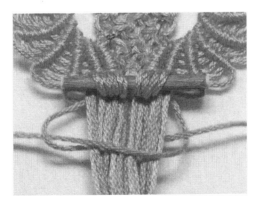

Step 53: Tie the strong knot behind your owl and cut the excessive edges. And you're done!

CONCLUSION

Taking an ordinary regular room and changing it into a room that will stun guests is the fantasy of most homeowners. The utilization of art, made with macramé hitches, is an extraordinary method to accomplish this fantasy. The artwork you place in your home should say something regarding you and your character. With such a large number of decisions of artwork finished with macramé ties, there is no uncertainty that you can discover something that coordinates your character and style. Interestingly, every one of these centerpieces is high quality, so they are each one of a kind of creation and makes certain to astonish your visitor whenever they go into your home.

The craftsman making this art utilizes these various materials to wrap bottles and chime ringers and make floor mats, napkins, needle cases, and so forth. With the variety of materials utilized, it isn't elusive things made with macramé knots to arrange with any stylistic theme you have in your home. These artwork pieces would then be able to be set in your home to include some extraordinary touches, particularly any life with a nautical stylistic theme.

It is ideal to have designs that can complement any retire, bar, or wall. Wouldn't a Rum jug secure with macramé hitches look multiple times better sitting on a bar or rack than the regular old, boring container? Envision you pour a beverage for a visitor from a cord secured bottle, at that point give them their beverage to put on a liner made of cord, this after they strolled into your home and cleaned their feet on your floor mat made of the cord also. At long last, a home stylistic layout that is genuinely exceptional, and now the Jones will stay aware of you rather than the reverse way around. What we as a whole need is a room with an excellent point of convergence, and art made with macramé knots will make that point of convergence in any room. All these complicated pieces of art will add a feeling to your space, and individuals will need to know where you got them from, whenever you purchase artwork to brighten your home, recollect that Macramé Knots are not your grandma art any longer.

The beauty of Macramé as a vintage art that has survived extinction for centuries and has continued to thrive as a technique of choice for making sophisticated but straight-forward items is simply unrivaled. The simple fact that you have decided to read this manual means that you are well on your way to making something great. There is truly a certain, unequaled feeling of satisfaction that comes from crafting your own masterpiece.

The most important rule in Macramé is the maxim: "Practice makes perfect." If you cease to practice constantly, your skills are likely to deteriorate over time. So, keep your skills sharp, exercise the creative parts of your brain, and keep creating mind-blowing handmade masterpieces. Jewelry and fashion accessories made with even the most basic Macramé knots are always a beauty to behold. Hence they serve as perfect gifts for loved ones on special occasions. Presenting a Macramé bracelet to someone, for instance, passes the message that you didn't just remember to get them a gift, you also treasure them so much that you chose to invest your time into crafting something unique especially for them too, and trust me, that is a very powerful message. However, the most beautiful thing about Macramé is perhaps the fact that it helps to create durable items. Hence you can keep a piece of decoration, or a fashion accessory you made for yourself for many years, enjoy the value, and still feel nostalgic anytime you remember when you made it. It even feels better when you made that item with someone. This feature of durability also makes Macramé accessories incredibly perfect gifts.

Macramé can also serve as an avenue for you to begin your small dream business. After perfecting your Macramé skills, you can conveniently sell your items and get paid well for your products, especially if you can perfectly make items like bracelets that people buy a lot. You could even train people and start your own little company that makes bespoke

Macramé fashion accessories. The opportunities that Macramé presents are truly endless.

There you have it, everything you need to know to get you started with your own macramé knots. This is going to show you just how easy it is to get started in this hobby, and once you get the hang of things, you are going to find that it is easier than ever to get started with your own projects.

So, stay sharp, keep practicing, and keep getting better. Welcome to a world of infinite possibilities!

Manufactured by Amazon.ca
Bolton, ON